Original title:
Chill and Charm

Copyright © 2024 Swan Charm
All rights reserved.

Author: Liina Liblikas
ISBN HARDBACK: 978-9916-79-963-5
ISBN PAPERBACK: 978-9916-79-964-2
ISBN EBOOK: 978-9916-79-965-9

Echoes of Serenity in Nature's Heart

In the whispering trees, calm winds sigh,
Soft shadows dance as the birds fly by.
Gentle streams hum their soothing tune,
Beneath the gaze of a silver moon.

Mountains stand tall, draped in mist,
Embracing the silence, nature's kiss.
A symphony plays in the rustling leaves,
A melody that the spirit believes.

Sunlight filters through a leafy dome,
Where wildflowers sway, and the heart finds home.
Each heartbeat echoes with the earth's breath,
In harmony's cradle, there is no death.

In the deep woods where the soul can roam,
Time holds still, creating a poem.
With every footstep on soft, mossy ground,
Eternal peace in nature is found.

As twilight descends in hues of gold,
Stories of nature quietly unfold.
In each fleeting moment, love's light shines,
A boundless connection through tangled vines.

Radiant Dreams on Lazy Days

Soft sunlight spills on fields so wide,
Waves of golden warmth collide.
In the shade, our laughter sings,
As the gentle breeze takes wings.

Clouds like cotton drift so slow,
Painting pictures down below.
In these moments, dreams will play,
Filling hearts on lazy days.

Gentle Murmurs of a Quiet Grove

In the grove, where shadows dance,
   Nature sings a soft romance.
   Whispers echo, secrets told,
  In this haven, hearts unfold.

Leaves above sway in delight,
Crickets chirp as day turns night.
 Every sound a soothing balm,
In this grove, the world feels calm.

Secrets of the Whispering Pines

Beneath the pines, where stillness reigns,
Ancient secrets hide in chains.
Rustling branches share their lore,
Lost in time, forevermore.

Scent of pine and earth combine,
Nature's gift, a pure design.
In the heart of woods so deep,
Lies the magic, ours to keep.

Tranquil Waves in a Sunlit Bay

Waves cascade with gentle grace,
Sunlight sparkles, nature's lace.
Seagulls call from skies so bright,
In this scene, all feels right.

Sandy shores invite our feet,
Where ocean's pulse and heartbeat meet.
In this bay, our worries sway,
Lost in peace, come what may.

Soft Songs of the Setting Sun

Whispers of twilight kiss the sky,
Brushstrokes of amber passing by.
As day bows low to night's embrace,
Soft melodies echo in this space.

Clouds painted gold, a gentle sigh,
The world rests still, as shadows fly.
Crickets sing their evening tune,
While stars awake beneath the moon.

Nature's Palette in Pastel Hues

Blossoms bloom with grace anew,
Petals glisten with morning dew.
Colors dance in the warm sunlight,
A symphony of flora, pure delight.

Birds flutter through the open air,
Echoing songs of love and care.
Leaves swirl down like confetti rain,
Nature's artistry, a vivid refrain.

Revel in the Beauty of Simple Things

A cup of tea on a rainy day,
Laughter shared, worries drift away.
Warmth of friendship, a sweet embrace,
In life's small joys, we find our place.

The rustle of leaves in the soft breeze,
Sunshine breaking through the trees.
Moments cherished, time taken slow,
In simple scenes, our hearts do grow.

Inhalations of Peace

Breathe in deeply, fill your soul,
The world around begins to roll.
Gentle waves caress the shore,
A tranquil heart forever more.

Mountains stand in quiet grace,
Time slows down in nature's space.
Inhale calmness, let it flow,
In every breath, let worries go.

Exhalations of Joy

Release the laughter, let it soar,
Echoing love from every pore.
Each giggle shared, a gift bestowed,
In joyous moments, life is showed.

Swaying freely, dance with delight,
Twirl beneath the stars so bright.
With every exhale, find your cheer,
In simple pleasures, treasure here.

Moments of Magic in Wandering Thoughts

In the silence of a dream,
Whispers dance like silver streams.
Thoughts take flight on wings of night,
Crafting stories, pure delight.

Every shadow, every light,
Paints a picture, soft and bright.
Moments linger, time stands still,
Magic hidden in a thrill.

Voices echo, soft and clear,
Guiding whispers, drawing near.
In the maze of thought and maze,
Life unfolds in gentle ways.

Memories wrapped in twilight hues,
Chasing stars, the heart renews.
In this space where dreams entwine,
Wandering thoughts become divine.

Catch the moments, hold them tight,
In the heart, they burn so bright.
Magic sparkles in each glance,
Wandering thoughts, a timeless dance.

Daydreams Wrapped in Soft Feathers

Floating on a soft, sweet cloud,
Daydreams whisper, soft and loud.
Wrapped in warmth of feathery light,
Thoughts take flight into the night.

Gentle breezes kiss the skin,
Inviting peace to dwell within.
Every moment feels so rare,
Daydreams drift through fragrant air.

Silken threads of hopes and dreams,
Woven in with flowing streams.
Time dissolves in golden rays,
Caught in the light of endless days.

With each breath, the spirit soars,
Unlocking wide, unseen doors.
In these dreams, the heart finds grace,
Soft feathers, a warm embrace.

Cherished visions softly glide,
In the world where dreams abide.
Wrapped in magic, still and free,
Daydreams dance in harmony.

Easy Breezes and Sunlit Glimmers

Underneath the azure skies,
Breezes weave in playful ties.
Sunlit glimmers set the scene,
Nature's canvas, vivid green.

Whispers of the leaves, so fair,
Secrets hidden in the air.
Every rustle tells a tale,
In the soft and gentle gale.

Golden rays on petals sing,
Celebrating what daylight brings.
Easy moments, time to share,
Breezy laughter fills the air.

With each step on grassy ground,
Colors dance, and joy is found.
In the light, we find our way,
Chasing dreams through brightened day.

Joyful echoes fill the heart,
Nature's wonders, purest art.
Easy breezes guide us home,
Sunlit glimmers, never alone.

The Art of Resting in Nature's Lap

In the quiet of the wood,
Nature speaks where stillness stood.
Softly resting, breath aligns,
Lost in peace, the spirit shines.

Beneath the branches, cool and wide,
Thoughts meander, tucked inside.
Each soft whisper calls our name,
In this cradle, wild and tame.

Leaves fluttering in the light,
Dancing shadows, pure delight.
Time dissolves in gentle sighs,
As the world slows, calm replies.

Resting here, the heart beats slow,
Finding balance, letting go.
Nature's lap, a soothing grace,
In her arms, we find our place.

Breathe in deep this sacred ground,
In her calm, all joy is found.
The art of resting, truly grand,
Nature holds us, hand in hand.

Harmony in a Whispered Breeze

In the stillness, nature sighs,
Gentle whispers float on high.
Leaves converse in quiet tones,
As peace settles in gentle zones.

Clouds drift softly, dreams take flight,
Colors dance in morning light.
The world listens, heart aglow,
Feeling all that breezes know.

A song of life in every wave,
Each note a wish, each sound a crave.
In harmony, the heart finds grace,
Breath of earth, a warm embrace.

Birds above in perfect flight,
Chasing shadows, fading light.
Together in the vast expanse,
A symphony in nature's dance.

Let the whispers fill the air,
Gather beauty, everywhere.
In each moment, find your ease,
Life is woven in the breeze.

Driftwood Dreams by the Shore

On sandy shores where dreams are cast,
Old driftwood rests, memories vast.
Each grain of sand, a story shared,
Waves compose a song, ensnared.

Tides that surge and gently pull,
Whispers echo, hearts are full.
Starlit nights, where wishes flow,
A canvas painted by the glow.

Moonlit paths that lead us near,
Every shadow holds a cheer.
Footprints soft on fragile ground,
A world of silence all around.

Seagulls cry, the ocean's hymn,
A tranquil tune, a night so dim.
Amongst the shells, reflections gleam,
We find our ease in twilight's dream.

With every wave, the past renews,
The shore tells tales of love and blues.
In driftwood dreams, we come alive,
Where every heart is free to thrive.

A Tapestry of Soft Hues

In gardens bright, colors meld,
Petals whisper, secrets held.
Softest pinks and blues entwine,
Nature's palette, truly divine.

Golden dawns and twilight's grace,
Every shade finds its place.
Brush of wind, a gentle hand,
Painting life across the land.

Clouds like cotton, floating high,
Catching dreams as they drift by.
In the sunset's warm embrace,
Every hue a soft, sweet trace.

Silken threads in the moon's glow,
Crafting stories only we know.
With each heartbeat, colors sing,
Life's rich tapestry take wing.

Embrace the light, the shadow dance,
Every moment, given chance.
In soft hues, find peace anew,
A journey wrapped in vibrant view.

Moonbeam Reflections

Under a sky of deep navy blue,
Moonlight spills, a silvery hue.
Casting dreams on the quiet ground,
In the night, magic is found.

Rippling waters, secrets sway,
Quiet whispers lead the way.
Stars above in a cosmic trance,
Shimmer softly, a soulful dance.

Stillness wraps the world in grace,
Each heartbeat finds a sacred place.
Moments linger, time stands still,
In moonbeam dreams, we seek to fill.

Echoes dance on the gentle tide,
In the glow, our hopes abide.
Shadows waltz in moonlit streams,
Carrying forth our whispered dreams.

As dawn approaches, light will break,
In its warmth, new paths we take.
Yet in the night, our spirits soar,
Finding peace forevermore.

Enigmas of the Night's Embrace

Whispers float on cool night air,
Stars like secrets everywhere,
Shadows dance with hidden grace,
Mysteries in each dark space.

Moonlight bathes the silent trees,
Rustling leaves, a gentle breeze,
Time stands still, a fleeting sigh,
Underneath the velvet sky.

Footsteps echo on the ground,
Where echoes of the night resound,
Stories linger, tales untold,
In the night, the heart is bold.

The clock ticks softly, time won't win,
In this realm, life's whispers spin,
Every shadow holds a spark,
Igniting dreams within the dark.

As dawn creeps in, the spells may fade,
But the night's secrets won't degrade,
In our hearts, they hold their place,
Enigmas of the night's embrace.

The Beauty of Unrushed Moments

In the stillness, time unfolds,
Each heartbeat softly molds,
A gentle pause amidst the rush,
Where life's colors start to blush.

Breath by breath, we savor grace,
In the quiet, find our space,
Like petals opening at dawn,
Unrushed moments linger on.

A smile shared, a hand to hold,
In these moments, love is bold,
Weave our dreams in golden threads,
Count the stars above our heads.

Nature sings a tender tune,
Beneath the silver crescent moon,
Every second, pure delight,
In the warmth of soft twilight.

So let time slip, like grains of sand,
In the embrace of life, we stand,
For in stillness, we will find,
The beauty of an unhurried mind.

Soft Footsteps on Dewy Grass

Morning breaks with softest light,
Dewdrops shimmer, pure and bright,
Footsteps trace a gentle line,
Through the meadow, fresh and fine.

Whispers of the waking breeze,
Flowing through the verdant trees,
Each blade dances in the sun,
A new day has now begun.

Nature's paintbrush strokes the scene,
Colors vibrant, lush, and green,
With each step, the earth awakes,
In the calm, my spirit breaks.

Echoes of a tranquil sound,
In this moment, peace is found,
Life's soft pulse beneath the skies,
In the heart, the wonder lies.

So I tread on dewy grass,
In the quiet, I will pass,
Finding joy in simple things,
Where nature's soul forever sings.

Twilight's Embrace of Solitude

As the sun dips low and fades,
Twilight casts its gentle shades,
In the quiet, silence speaks,
Solitude, the heart it seeks.

Colors blend in soft array,
End of light, the close of day,
Every moment holds its breath,
In twilight's arms, we find our depth.

Stars begin to stretch and yawn,
Night unfolds like a soft lawn,
Dreams awaken in the dark,
Guiding paths with each small spark.

Lonely hearts in shadows roam,
Yet in darkness, we find home,
Comfort found in gentle night,
Embraced by starlit, silver light.

So let the world in silence sleep,
In twilight's arms, our secrets keep,
For in this still, serene ballet,
We discover ourselves, come what may.

The Gentle Rush of a Stream

The water flows with grace,
A melody so clear,
Each ripple tells a tale,
Of moments held so dear.

Smooth stones lie in repose,
Glistening in the sun,
Nature's purest embrace,
A quiet place to run.

The laughter of the leaves,
Dances with the breeze,
A symphony of life,
In perfect harmonies.

Beneath the arching sky,
Reflections softly gleam,
In this tranquil retreat,
I find my whispered dream.

The journey never ends,
Through valleys lush and wide,
With every gentle turn,
I walk the stream's sweet side.

Harmonies of a Serene Evening

The sun dips low and slow,
As shadows start to blend,
A canvas painted soft,
The night is on the mend.

Crickets sing their sweet song,
A choir of the dusk,
Notes drift on the cool air,
In twilight's gentle husk.

Stars appear like jewels,
In the blanket of night,
Each one a twinkling wish,
A beacon of pure light.

The world feels still and calm,
A pause in life's great race,
As moonlight bathes the earth,
In serene, soft embrace.

Time flows on like water,
A rhythm so divine,
In this evening's hush,
My heart begins to shine.

Soft Light Through the Branches

The morning light creeps in,
With rays that softly dance,
Through branches intertwined,
In nature's fleeting glance.

A whisper of the dawn,
Caresses every leaf,
Awakening the world,
In warmth beyond belief.

Golden hues adorn,
The forest's quiet face,
As shadows gently wane,
In this sacred space.

The songbirds greet the day,
With melodies so sweet,
In this embrace of light,
All life feels so complete.

The breezes weave a tale,
Of moments fresh and bright,
As I wander slowly,
In the soft morning light.

Elegance in the Dappled Shade

Beneath the ancient trees,
A carpet green and cool,
The sunlight breaks in shards,
Where shadows gently pool.

Each leaf a work of art,
With patterns bold and bright,
The dappled shade invites,
A moment to delight.

The air is filled with peace,
A sanctuary grand,
Where whispers of the past,
Are held in nature's hand.

In this quiet haven,
Thoughts wander, time stands still,
As nature's gentle hand,
Fulfills the heart's great will.

The elegance of green,
Breathes magic all around,
In dappled shade I find,
A solace deeply found.

Peaceful Ramblings Under the Stars

Under a velvet sky so wide,
Whispers of the night abide.
Dreams unfurl like sails in flight,
Guided by the silver light.

Footsteps soft upon the grass,
Time drifts by, a fleeting pass.
Each star a story yet to tell,
In this quiet magic, dwell.

Moonbeams dance on water's edge,
Nature sings a sacred pledge.
In the stillness, hearts align,
Lost in thoughts both pure and fine.

Crickets serenade the night,
Echoes of the past take flight.
With every breath, a sense of peace,
As worries fade, and troubles cease.

Beneath the cosmos, dreams ignite,
In endless depths of soft twilight.
We'll wander on 'til morning's rise,
Bound by love beneath the skies.

Soft Breezes and Gentle Whispers

Soft breezes caress the trees,
Carrying secrets with such ease.
A gentle touch upon the skin,
Where earth and sky both meet within.

Whispers float through fragrant air,
Nature's song beyond compare.
Each note a soft, inviting call,
An echo of the world, so small.

Sunlight filters through the leaves,
Dancing shadows weave and cleave.
Beneath the boughs, life sways and spins,
A tapestry where love begins.

Flowing streams murmur their tale,
In perfect rhythm, never stale.
With every step, the heart finds grace,
In this warm and sacred space.

Together let us breathe the air,
In harmony, a love we share.
With soft breezes and whispered dreams,
We'll find ourselves, or so it seems.

Enchanted Evenings by the Shore

Waves kiss the sand with gentle grace,
Under the moon's soft, silver face.
Each ripple tells a tale untold,
In the night's embrace, pure and bold.

Stars sprinkled like diamonds in the dark,
Illuminating paths to embark.
Footprints washed away by the tide,
Yet memories linger, side by side.

The briny air, a breath of peace,
As worries fade and moments cease.
Laughter mingles with ocean's song,
In this place where we belong.

Seagulls glide through the twilight haze,
In the stillness, our hearts ablaze.
With every wave, dreams intertwine,
Here by the shore, your hand in mine.

As the world fades into slumber,
We cherish time, letting it encumber.
In enchanted evenings, love adorned,
Forever more, our hearts reborn.

Serene Moments in Twilight

Twilight descends in hues of gold,
A canvas where day meets night, bold.
Soft shadows stretch and yawn with ease,
Nature whispers secrets in the breeze.

Crickets chirp their evening tune,
As the stars awaken, one by one soon.
In this quiet hour, dreams take flight,
Time stands still, bathed in soft light.

The world transforms, both calm and bright,
In serene moments, hearts unite.
Each heartbeat echoes with a sigh,
Underneath the vast, open sky.

Gentle winds weave through the trees,
A serenade of whispered pleas.
As twilight wraps us in its arms,
We find comfort in nature's charms.

With every breath, we slow the race,
Embracing time, in love's warm embrace.
In serene moments, let us stay,
For in this light, we find our way.

Etherial Walks Through the Forest

Sunlight filters through the leaves,
A gentle rustle in the trees.
Whispers float on soft, cool breeze,
Nature's dance brings hearts at ease.

Shadows linger, shapes are cast,
Footsteps soft on mossy ground.
In this realm, time is surpassed,
A secret world, so profound.

Flowers bloom in colors bright,
Sparkling dew on blades of grass.
Birds take flight in pure delight,
Moments here are meant to last.

Ancient trunks stand tall and wise,
Guardians of tales untold.
Beneath their boughs, dreams arise,
Memories in silence mold.

Through the woods, a path unwinds,
Each turn unveils a new surprise.
Echoes sweetly join in kind,
A melody that never dies.

The Subdued Delight of Sunset

The sky ignites in hues of gold,
Soft tendrils of light start to wane.
Whispers of dusk, a story told,
As day succumbs to night's sweet reign.

The horizon bleeds in crimson fire,
Clouds painted with violet grace.
Nature bows to the stars' choir,
In twilight's arms, we find our place.

Birds find rest as shadows grow,
The whispering trees start to sway.
The evening's charm begins to flow,
In this stillness, thoughts drift away.

The cool breeze brings a subtle sigh,
Echoes of laughter linger near.
As night ascends, the world goes dry,
Yet in the stars, dreams reappear.

The day retreats, the moon takes flight,
With gentle touch, it lights the way.
In the soft embrace of night,
We find ourselves in calm array.

Hushed Conversations with Nature

In the meadow where wildflowers sway,
The breeze carries secrets untold.
Nature speaks in its own sweet way,
With whispers of wonder, pure gold.

A brook babbles under a veil of leaves,
Its gentle laughter fills the air.
In tranquil moments, the heart believes,
There's wisdom hidden everywhere.

The rustle of grass, a soft reply,
As insects waltz on fragile wings.
In silence, the soul learns how to fly,
In the symphony that nature sings.

The mountains stand in stoic grace,
Guardians of the stories we share.
They cradle dreams in their embrace,
A testament to time laid bare.

As shadows lengthen, day takes flight,
Night's cool canvas begins to spread.
In these hushed chats, we find delight,
In the beauty of words unspoken.

The Quietude of Hidden Places

There lies a glen where silence sings,
Where time holds still and hearts can breathe.
In secret nooks, the world unwinds,
Revealing beauty weaves beneath.

Cascading streams in crystal hues,
Their murmurs soft, a lullaby.
Beneath the trees, the soft light brews,
A canvas painted by passing sky.

Mossy stones invite gentle touch,
Whispers of earth beneath our feet.
In quiet places, we find so much,
The heart discovers its rhythmic beat.

Ferns unfurl like nature's grace,
Guarded thoughts begin to unfurl.
In hidden realms, we find our place,
Where peace and solace gently swirl.

As twilight deepens, shadows play,
The world outside fades far away.
In quietude, our souls align,
In hushed embraces, we intertwine.

Breezy Serenades of Solitude

In whispers soft, the breezes sigh,
They weave through trees, where shadows lie.
A playful dance upon a stream,
In solitude, I find my dream.

The rustling leaves, a sweet refrain,
Each note a balm for whispered pain.
Alone but not in silence deep,
These breezy songs, my heart they keep.

A lonesome path through fields of gold,
In nature's arms, my story's told.
The sky above, a canvas wide,
In solitude, I'm not denied.

The gentle touch of wind so light,
It carries hopes into the night.
With every breath, I tune my ear,
To breezy serenades I hold dear.

A moment's peace, a fleeting grace,
In solitude, I find my place.
These whispered melodies of old,
In breezy tales, my heart unfolds.

Lullabies of the Moonlit Sea

The moonlight dances on the waves,
A lullaby my spirit craves.
Soft whispers in the ocean's sigh,
Guiding dreams as they drift by.

Stars above, like lanterns glow,
Each twinkle brings a tale to flow.
The water hums a gentle tune,
Beneath the watchful, silver moon.

A fishing boat, its lantern bright,
Sails softly into the night.
With every splash, a soothing sound,
In this embrace, my calm is found.

The night is draped in velvet skies,
With sleepy waves, the ocean sighs.
These lullabies, a soft caress,
In moonlit dreams, I find my rest.

The tide rolls in, a gentle plea,
To sail away and simply be.
In every wave, a love song flows,
A lullaby that always knows.

Delicate Dance of Dewdrops

At dawn's first light, the world awakes,
With dewdrops fine on blades they make.
A delicate dance in sunlight's kiss,
Each sparkle holds a moment's bliss.

In grassy fields, the jewels play,
Their twinkling path lights up the day.
Soft whispers on the morning breeze,
Each droplet sings with joyful ease.

They gather close on petals bright,
In unity, they catch the light.
A fleeting glimpse of nature's art,
In every drop, a story starts.

As sun ascends and shadows fade,
These dewdrops glisten, memories made.
In brief embrace, they vanish near,
Yet in my heart, they hold me dear.

The delicate dance of daybreak's grace,
In each small sphere, life's beauty trace.
So cherish now these moments rare,
For dewdrops' dance is beyond compare.

Warm Embrace of Autumn Leaves

In autumn's grasp, the colors spree,
A tapestry of gold and tree.
Leaves flutter down, a gentle sigh,
In nature's arms, time flows by.

They gather round, a carpet made,
In rustling whispers, memories laid.
With every step, a crunching song,
In warm embrace, where I belong.

The air is crisp, the sunlight warm,
In golden hues, the world transforms.
A fleeting dance in soft decay,
In autumn's glow, I long to stay.

Each leaf a story, rich and bold,
In vibrant shades that never grow old.
They fall but promise to regain,
In cycles sweet, life's sweet refrain.

So gather close, and hold them tight,
These autumn leaves, a pure delight.
In their embrace, I find my peace,
In warmest hues, my soul's release.

Dreamy Vistas of a Slow Afternoon

In the light of the afternoon glow,
Fields stretch wide, where soft winds blow.
Clouds drift slowly, like dreams untold,
In the warmth of the sun, all is gold.

Birds hum sweetly, a gentle tune,
While shadows dance beneath the moon.
Time feels lighter, as moments slip,
On this voyage, let my spirit sip.

The horizon paints in colors so bright,
Echoing joy in the fading light.
Every heartbeat syncs with the air,
In this wonderland, free from care.

Whispers of dreams wrap around my heart,
In this serene canvas, I play my part.
Nature's embrace feels warm and near,
In the essence of life, nothing to fear.

Whispers of the Breeze Through Blooms

Petals flutter on soft, sweet sighs,
Where the sun kisses earth, the spirit flies.
Gentle whispers in a garden grand,
Each bloom cradles secrets of the land.

Bees hum lightly in an endless dance,
Gathering nectar in a blissful trance.
The fragrance drifts on a tender breeze,
Carrying laughter, calming all unease.

Colors burst in a vibrant spree,
Nature's palette, wild and free.
Each moment blossoms, a fresh delight,
In the embrace of the day, so bright.

The wind speaks softly, a playful tease,
Through the meadow, among the trees.
As life flows by, I pause to see,
The whispers of the breeze, a joyous plea.

Reflections on a Calm Lake

Still waters mirror the vast blue sky,
Where dreams linger, and silence sighs.
Ripples fade in gentle embrace,
Time slows down, in this sacred space.

Canoes glide like whispers in time,
Embracing shadows that softly rhyme.
Clouds float lazily, drifting on high,
In this moment, I learn to fly.

The trees stand watch, with secrets to share,
Guardians of memories, tender and rare.
Each ripple a story, each wave a song,
In the heart of nature, where I belong.

Underneath, the depths hold mysteries true,
Life's reflections, a tranquil view.
In solitude's grace, I find my way,
In the calm of the lake, I long to stay.

Swaying Grass and Distant Laughter

The grass sways gently in playful cheer,
Beneath a dome where skies are clear.
Laughter echoes through fields of green,
In every note, pure joy is seen.

Children run wild, their spirits soar,
With every giggle, hearts crave more.
The sun is a friend, casting warm rays,
In this tapestry of bright summer days.

Butterflies dance on a whispering breeze,
Nature joins in with harmony's ease.
Time stands still; in these moments, I find,
The simple treasures of life intertwined.

Under the blue, we chase and play,
Swaying grass leads us on our way.
In the laughter that fills the sweet air,
Every heartbeat reflects love's care.

The Caress of a Soft Breeze

Whispers through the willow trees,
Gentle hands of summer's breeze.
Leaves dance lightly in the air,
Nature's breath, a tender care.

Kisses on the flowers bright,
Painting petals with pure light.
Echoes of a soft refrain,
Serenity in every grain.

Golden sun begins to set,
Casting shadows we won't forget.
Cooling whispers on our skin,
A tranquil world, peace within.

Underneath the fading sky,
Breeze will linger, softly sigh.
Awakening the night so still,
In the hush, our hearts will fill.

Crickets chirp, a lullaby,
While the stars begin to fly.
In the dark, a soothing song,
In the heart, we all belong.

Hidden Wonders of the Meadow

Where the wildflowers sway and shine,
Secrets hide in nature's design.
Colors blaze beneath the sun,
Every petal, a story spun.

Butterflies flit, grace in their flight,
Dewdrops glisten, jewels of light.
Rabbits play in whispered grass,
Moments fleeting, like time will pass.

In the hush, a brook does flow,
Softly singing tales we know.
Nestled beneath a leafy shade,
Dreams unfold, adventures made.

The gentle rustle, nature's tune,
Morning's blush, the rising moon.
Every shadow tells a tale,
In this haven, none will pale.

Children laugh, they run and roam,
In this meadow, they find a home.
Hidden wonders, simple joys,
Nature's heart, the world's toys.

Radiance in Stillness

Amidst the calm, a light so bright,
Illuminates the quiet night.
Stars like diamonds, softly gleam,
Filling the world with a dream.

Moonbeams dance on tranquil lakes,
Whispers flow as daylight breaks.
In the stillness, hearts align,
Finding solace, pure divine.

Echoes of the day recede,
Crickets sing, a soothing creed.
Night enfolds us, wrapped in grace,
In this moment, we find our place.

Candles flicker, shadows play,
Warmth surrounds at the close of day.
Radiance glows in peaceful minds,
In stillness, hope forever binds.

Every breath, a sacred vow,
In the now, we cherish how.
Eyes closed tight, we drift and sway,
In radiance, we find our way.

The Magic of a Subtle Glow

In the twilight's tender embrace,
A gentle glow lights up the space.
Flickers dance in leaves above,
A whispered hint of hidden love.

Fireflies weave through night's cool air,
Magic sparkles everywhere.
Softly glowing, spirits rise,
Awakening the night's surprise.

Waves of light in silent streams,
Carrying our hopes and dreams.
In their flicker, stories weave,
In the dark, we still believe.

Warmth within the tender night,
Guided by that soft, sweet light.
Every heart, a glowing ember,
In the dark, we all remember.

So let the magic gently flow,
Through every heart, a subtle glow.
In that light, our spirits grow,
Together in the night's sweet show.

The Comfort of Familiar Paths

Beneath the trees where shadows play,
I wander where my heart feels safe.
Each step on this well-trodden way,
Brings whispers of the past, a waif.

The breeze it hums a gentle tune,
Through leaves that dance and sway so free.
I find my peace beneath the moon,
This quiet space, just me and me.

Paved in dreams and memories bright,
The path I walk is filled with light.
Each corner holds a story near,
A cherished thought, a moment dear.

With every step, I feel the ground,
That knows my soul, its every sigh.
In this embrace, I am unbound,
A wanderer beneath the sky.

And though the world may shift and change,
These familiar paths, they guide me still.
In every twist, in every range,
I find my heart, I find my will.

Delicate Notes of Nature's Song

In morning light, on dew-kissed leaves,
Soft whispers float on gentle air.
Nature sings, and the heart believes,
In harmony beyond compare.

A rustling breeze through fragrant blooms,
Carries melodies so pure and sweet.
As sunlight dances in the rooms,
Of every flower, all hearts meet.

The brook's soft babble forms a line,
Between the silence and the sound.
With every note, the world aligns,
In music grand, where peace is found.

As twilight falls, the crickets play,
Their symphony in evening's glow.
Each chirp a promise, night will stay,
In nature's song, our spirits grow.

With every breath, the earth reveals,
A world alive with subtle grace.
In nature's notes, the heart heals,
In every sound, a warm embrace.

Sweet Encounters in the Dusk

The sun dips low, a painted sky,
Gold and amber fill the night.
In shadows soft, sweet dreams drift by,
With whispers shared in fading light.

A gentle breeze wraps 'round my skin,
Bringing secrets of the day.
In twilight hours, new tales begin,
As stars awake, to softly play.

I stroll through gardens kissed by dusk,
Where flowers nod and leave their scent.
In every bloom, a hint of musk,
A fleeting moment, time well spent.

Two souls may chance to share a glance,
Amongst the blooms, beneath the stars.
A fleeting smile, a whispered chance,
In every heart, a longing spars.

As darkness falls, the world feels still,
In quiet corners, dreams convene.
With every breath, the night fulfills,
Sweet encounters, gentle and keen.

The Softness of a Distant Melody

Across the hills, a faint refrain,
Drifts through the air, a soothing sound.
It dances lightly, calls my name,
In every note, my heart is bound.

From distant lands, the echoes play,
A lullaby that calls to me.
In twilight's glow, it leads the way,
Through softest dreams, I long to be.

The cadence flows like water clear,
With every wave, my spirit soars.
A timeless song that draws me near,
To hidden shores, to distant doors.

Each note a feather, light and pure,
That whispers secrets of the night.
In harmony, my heart is sure,
In every sound, a journey's flight.

With distant echoes as my guide,
I wander on this path of grace.
In music's arms, I will abide,
In every note, I find my place.

Tender Embraces in the Light

In morning's glow we find our way,
With whispers soft, we choose to stay.
The warmth surrounds, a gentle touch,
In these sweet moments, we feel so much.

Your laughter dances on the breeze,
A melody that puts my heart at ease.
In every glance, a spark ignites,
Tender embraces in soft twilight.

Through fields of daisies, hand in hand,
We wander freely, on golden sand.
With every step, the world seems right,
As we lose ourselves in the light.

The shadows fade, the worries cease,
With you I find my perfect peace.
In your embrace, time stands still,
A magic moment, a cherished thrill.

Together under the endless skies,
We paint our dreams, where love never dies.
In this embrace, forever strong,
We'll write our story, our own sweet song.

A Palette of Quiet Colors

Upon the canvas, strokes are light,
With quiet hues that glow at night.
Each shade whispers a secret tune,
Inviting peace beneath the moon.

Blues of calm, and greens of peace,
In this quiet world, I find my lease.
With every shade, a story told,
In colors soft, both warm and bold.

A touch of gold, a dash of gray,
Each moment crafted, day by day.
The beauty lies in the tender blend,
A living portrait that will not end.

With brush in hand, I lose all fears,
In vivid dreams, I shed my tears.
A tranquil landscape, so divine,
A palette of love; your heart is mine.

In silence, colors start to fade,
Yet memories of joy are made.
A legacy of heartbeats shared,
In this quiet space, we've dared.

With every layer, life's refrain,
We chase the sun, we dance in rain.
Together, we create our art,
A masterpiece born from the heart.

Cloud Dreams and Soft Realities

Floating softly, where dreams collide,
In silver clouds, we take our ride.
With every breath, fantasies rise,
Creating worlds beyond the skies.

In gentle whispers, secrets kept,
Among the clouds, where hope has leapt.
A tapestry of thoughts unfurled,
A dance of colors in our world.

Below, the earth calls out our names,
While up above, we chase our flames.
In this realm where visions soar,
We find the paths we've longed for.

Soft realities weave through our dreams,
With every moment, nothing's as it seems.
In each embrace, time fades away,
As we drift on through the day.

The fabric of life's sweet embrace,
In every heartbeat, a sacred space.
To find our way, in soaring heights,
Cloud dreams whisper of endless nights.

Together we'll float in this grand ballet,
Through soft realities, we'll find our way.
With hands entwined, we'll let life be,
In cloud dreams sweet, just you and me.

Constellations in a Serene Sky

Beneath the stars, a canvas wide,
We trace the paths where dreams reside.
With constellations guiding light,
We wander forth through magical night.

In velvet hues, each star a spark,
Whispering secrets in the dark.
We reach for stories long since told,
In cosmic wonders, hearts unfold.

Together we dance on the edge of time,
With every heartbeat, a rhythmic rhyme.
In this tranquil space, we dare to dream,
As moonlit beams cast silver gleam.

The universe wraps us in its grace,
In stellar light, we find our place.
With gentle hands, we paint the night,
Constellations of hope, shining bright.

In every twinkle, we'll find our way,
Through galaxies where love can sway.
A testament to all we share,
In the serene sky, beyond compare.

So let us wish upon these stars,
Together, we'll travel near and far.
With constellations as our guide,
In this vast sky, we'll abide.

A Waltz Among Delicate Petals

In gardens where soft colors sigh,
Petals twirl as breezes cry.
Nature's song, a sweet ballet,
A moment's grace that sweeps away.

Dancers bold, in softest hues,
They flutter gently, loving views.
Whispers of spring on each sweet breath,
Life renewed, escaping death.

As sunlight peeks through leafy trails,
Delicate tales in soft unveils.
They sway and bend to the soft air,
A waltz of joy beyond compare.

Each bloom a dream, ephemeral kiss,
In nature's arms, they find their bliss.
Together waltzing, hand in hand,
Lost in a sea of color grand.

The day dissolves, yet love remains,
In every dance, and all the gains.
Among delicate petals, hopes abide,
In this gentle waltz, we confide.

Shadows That Dance in Stillness

Shadows whisper on the ground,
In stillness, they are unbound.
Silent figures twist and sway,
Painting dreams, fading away.

Moonlight drapes a velvet cloak,
Nighttime's breath, a gentle stroke.
Ghostly forms in the cool air,
Waltzing softly, without a care.

Time stands still beneath the stars,
As shadows move beyond the scars.
Stories linger in the night,
Dancing lightly, taking flight.

In quiet corners, secrets thrive,
In moments where the heart's alive.
Each flicker tells a tale once told,
In dark's embrace, they unfold.

The dawn approaches, light draws near,
Yet shadows linger, still sincere.
A last dance before the sun,
In stillness, the shadows run.

The Warmth of Heartfelt Whispers

In the quiet of the night,
Soft whispers wrap us tight.
Words unspoken, softly shared,
In each heartbeat, love is bared.

Gentle sounds like summer rain,
Kiss the soul, erase the pain.
Voices mingle, soft and sweet,
In this moment, we complete.

Each word a spark, a flame ignites,
Flickering hopes in starry nights.
The warmth that comes from tender speech,
A bond so strong, it will not breach.

With every sigh that fills the air,
A promise builds, a love to share.
The power of love in every note,
In whispered dreams, our hearts float.

As dawn awakens, the whispers fade,
But memories linger, never trade.
A tapestry of love once spun,
In heartfelt whispers, we're as one.

Daydreams Among the Clouds

On lazy afternoons we drift,
In clouds that swirl and gently lift.
A canvas where our dreams reside,
In softest hues, we take a ride.

Floating high, we're free to roam,
Amidst the shapes that feel like home.
Each daydream paints a scene so bright,
Where fantasy embraces light.

A kingdom built on fleeting sighs,
With castles made of sweetened ties.
Where laughter echoes through the sky,
In daydreams, we can learn to fly.

Among the clouds, our hearts take flight,
In timeless worlds, everything feels right.
Suspended in this gentle grace,
Our worries fade, we find our place.

But as the sun begins to set,
We gather dreams we'll not forget.
In twilight's glow, we'll hold them tight,
Daydreams linger, a soft delight.

Velvet Nights and Distant Memories

Stars whisper secrets in the sky,
Soft shadows dance where dreams lie.
Each heartbeat echoes through the dark,
Fleeting moments leave their mark.

Moonlight glimmers on silent lakes,
Awakening old, forgotten wakes.
Memories swirl like leaves in flight,
Wrapped in the warmth of velvet night.

Whispers travel on the gentle breeze,
Carrying tales with such ease.
A touch of magic fills the air,
In distant memories, we repair.

Time stops still; we breathe the past,
In velvet nights that forever last.
A tapestry of both joy and sorrow,
Holds the promise of tomorrow.

So we linger, lost in thought,
Each memory treasured, never caught.
As velvet nights embrace our dreams,
Distant memories are more than they seem.

The Sweetness of Afternoon Tea

Leaves of green steep in porcelain white,
A gentle aroma drifts in delight.
Scones and cream, a delightful pair,
Sugar and laughter fill the air.

With every sip, time seems to pause,
In dainty cups, we find our cause.
Chatting softly beneath the sun,
Afternoon tea brings hearts as one.

Sunlight dances on the table's lace,
Each moment cherished, a warm embrace.
Flavors mingle, so rich, so bold,
In every story, a memory told.

Quiet conversations, smiles exchanged,
In the warmth of tea, we're rearranged.
A soothing balm for the restless soul,
The sweetness of tea makes us feel whole.

So let us gather, joyfully free,
In the simplicity of afternoon tea.
Together we savor, together we share,
Moments of sweetness beyond compare.

Serendipity in the Heart of Nature

Beneath the trees, a path unfolds,
Where whispers of nature are gently told.
A chance encounter with vibrant blooms,
In the heart of nature, life resumes.

Gentle streams bubble with laughter pure,
In serendipity, we find our cure.
Birds sing songs in harmonious flight,
Their melodies paint the morning light.

Wandering barefoot on soft, green grass,
Every moment a treasure, none shall pass.
Nature's embrace wraps us in peace,
In moments like this, our worries cease.

Clouds drift lazily across the blue,
In this sacred space, I find you.
Serendipity dances with every sigh,
In the heart of nature, we learn to fly.

Together we bask in the sun's warm glow,
Through the wild flowers, our spirits flow.
In every heartbeat, the wild invites,
Serendipity blooms in nature's lights.

Hushed Voices of a Lazy Stream

Flowing softly, the stream hums low,
Whispers of tales only rivers know.
Gentle ripples brush against the shore,
In the hushed voices, we long for more.

Moss-covered stones invite us to pause,
Nature's beauty deserves applause.
Sunlight winks through leaves overhead,
In quiet moments, our spirits are fed.

The air is laced with a fragrant breeze,
Carrying echoes of rustling trees.
With every turn, life unfolds anew,
In the lazy stream, dreams come into view.

Birds dart swiftly, a flash of wings,
Nature rejoices in the joy it brings.
Hushed voices call us to be still,
Embracing the calm, our hearts will fill.

As twilight approaches, shadows grow long,
The stream's soft song is a soothing throng.
In the hushed voices, we find our place,
Lost in the beauty, in nature's grace.

Notes of a Gentle Melody

Whispers of winds, soft and low,
Carrying dreams where flowers grow.
A lullaby sung by the trees,
Dancing leaves sway with such ease.

Echoes of laughter, pure delight,
In the stillness of peaceful night.
Softly strummed on heartstrings tight,
Melodies woven, taking flight.

Stars in the sky hum a tune,
Glowing softly, a silver moon.
Rhythms in shadows, gently creep,
Awakening souls from their sleep.

Moments of bliss, where time stands still,
In quiet corners, dreams we instill.
Harmonies intertwine with grace,
In this gentle, enchanted place.

Feel the music, let it flow,
Notes of kindness, let them grow.
Each heartbeat joins in the song,
Together we dance, where we belong.

A Touch of Lightness in Everyday Life

Morning's glow paints skies anew,
With golden beams and drops of dew.
Birds spin joy in vibrant flight,
A symphony of pure delight.

Coffee brews with warming cheer,
A fragrant hug, so close and near.
Laughter bubbles, coffee spills,
Simple moments, joy that thrills.

The breeze carries whispers sweet,
In gardens where the blossoms meet.
Children play, their spirits soar,
In every smile, joy we explore.

Raindrops play on window panes,
Creating songs of sweet refrains.
In the rhythm of daily grind,
A touch of lightness we will find.

At sunset's call, the world aglow,
To nature's canvas, we gladly go.
Each moment cherished, kind and bright,
In our hearts, we hold this light.

Patterns of Grace in Nature's Canvas

In the forest, shadows play,
Sunlight dances on leaves' array.
Petals scatter in the breeze,
Nature paints with gentle ease.

Rivers carve their paths so deep,
Drawing secrets that they keep.
Mountains stand in grand display,
Guarding dreams that drift away.

Waves cascade upon the shore,
Whispering tales of ages yore.
Stars above in a velvet sea,
Patterns of grace, wild and free.

The moon, a silver guiding light,
Watches over, embracing night.
Nature's brush strokes, bold and bright,
Remind us of life's pure delight.

In every bloom, in every breath,
Lies the beauty that conquers death.
In the silence, let us find,
The patterns of grace intertwined.

Sunshine Kisses on Gentle Waves

Golden rays touch the ocean's face,
As tides embrace in a sweet grace.
Children laugh by the sandy shore,
Building castles, dreaming more.

Seagulls dance in the warm, bright air,
With playful calls, joys we share.
Each wave whispers a gentle song,
Inviting hearts to belong.

Sunsets bleed in colors bold,
Painting stories yet untold.
Waves that shimmer in twilight's glow,
Carry wishes where the breezes blow.

Shells scattered, treasures from the sea,
Holding memories, wild and free.
In each ripple, a story flows,
Of summer days and soft repose.

When the day meets the stars above,
In the silence, we find our love.
Sunshine kisses and gentle waves,
In nature's arms, our spirit craves.

The Refinement of Fleeting Moments

In the shimmer of twilight's grace,
Time dances lightly, finds its place.
Each heartbeat whispers, soft and low,
A gentle reminder of what we know.

The clock ticks slowly, yet it's fast,
Moments like shadows, they do not last.
Yet within each laugh, a treasure lies,
In the ephemeral, the spirit flies.

Memories woven in golden thread,
Echoes of laughter, the things we said.
A glance, a touch, a fleeting sigh,
All captured moments as moments fly.

We chase the seconds, soft and sweet,
In every corner, where lives meet.
The art of being, the joy we find,
In fleeting moments, our souls entwined.

So let us savor, let us embrace,
The richness found in every space.
For in the dance of time we roam,
Fleeting moments, they lead us home.

Solace Among the Blossoms

In spring's embrace, the blossoms bloom,
Nature whispers, dispelling gloom.
Petals flutter, a soft ballet,
Finding peace at the end of the day.

The scent of jasmine fills the air,
A calming touch, a gentle care.
Beneath the branches, dreams take flight,
In the garden's heart, all feels right.

Colors burst in a vibrant show,
As the breeze carries soft songs low.
Each flower tells a story sweet,
Of solace found in the sun's retreat.

Time drifts slower as we stand still,
In nature's hush, we drink our fill.
Among the blossoms, storms subside,
We find our joy in the petals' glide.

So linger here, beneath the light,
In the blooming world, pure and bright.
For solace, dear, we do not seek,
Among the blossoms, our hearts speak.

Whispers of the Wandering Wind

The wind calls softly, secrets unfold,
Carrying tales that are centuries old.
It sweeps through valleys, over the hills,
Bringing whispers that the heart thrills.

In every rustle of leaves we find,
The stories hidden, tightly entwined.
Whispers of journeys lost and found,
On the canvas of life, they astound.

Through groves and meadows, it sings along,
A melody woven, a timeless song.
It dances fiercely and lightly glides,
Bringing with it the world's wild tides.

Listen closely, let your heart soar,
The wandering wind is forevermore.
In its embrace, we are set free,
Whispers of fate, pure poetry.

So close your eyes, breathe deep and learn,
From the wind's chorus, our spirits yearn.
In every gust, let memories blend,
As whispers of life around us wend.

Blush of Dawn's First Light

As the curtain lifts on night's retreat,
The blush of dawn paints the sky sweet.
Soft hues emerge, a gentle scene,
Waking the world with a tender sheen.

Birds stretch wings, with songs they greet,
The promise of day, an awakening treat.
Light dances on dew, a glistening lace,
In the quiet morn, we find our place.

Each sunbeam whispers of dreams anew,
Chasing the shadows, breaking through.
In the blush of dawn, hope takes flight,
A canvas of colors, pure delight.

Moments linger in the golden haze,
As the world begins its waking phase.
In the soft glow, our fears take flight,
Blush of dawn, a wondrous sight.

So rise with the sun, let your spirit soar,
Embrace the day, let your heart explore.
For in each dawn, life starts afresh,
In the blush of light, we find our flesh.

A Serenade for the Stars

In the hush of night, they gleam,
Whispers of dreams and silent beams.
Each twinkle paints the velvet sky,
A serenade where souls can fly.

Silver threads in a darkened loom,
Stories woven, dispel the gloom.
They beckon hearts to look and see,
The magic set in their decree.

Constellations dance with gentle grace,
Guiding travelers through time and space.
A lullaby in cosmic halls,
Where every wish and secret calls.

Infinite tales in a midnight glow,
The universe unfolds, a sacred show.
With every glance, a spark ignites,
A connection found in endless nights.

In twilight's embrace, we feel so small,
Yet in their light, we find our all.
A serenade for those who dream,
In the arms of stars, we softly beam.

Mellow Moments in the Garden

Morning dew on petals gleams,
Nature whispers soft, sweet dreams.
Bees hum tunes in blooms so bright,
A canvas painted in pure light.

Golden rays peer through the trees,
With gentle breezes that tease.
Each flower sways in playful dance,
Inviting all to take a chance.

A bench beneath the willow's shade,
Where time slows down, and worries fade.
In this embrace of earth and sky,
Mellow moments softly sigh.

Beneath a canopy of green,
The quietest joys are seen.
Birdsongs flutter through the air,
A melody beyond compare.

At twilight, colors blend and weave,
Nature's charm makes us believe.
In the garden's gentle grace,
We find a soothing, sacred space.

The Allure of Gentle Shadows

As daylight wanes, shadows grow,
Whispers of dusk in an evening glow.
Soft silhouettes begin to play,
In the twilight's warm array.

They cradle secrets of the night,
Where silence drapes in soft twilight.
A dance of forms, both bold and shy,
In gentle twilight, they softly lie.

The world slips into calm repose,
Where mystery within shadows grows.
Through branches high, the moonlight glows,
Embracing night, as stillness flows.

Whispers linger in the air,
A soft caress, a fleeting stare.
With every heartbeat, shadows blend,
In their allure, our worries mend.

As stars emerge, shadows retreat,
Leaving behind a quiet beat.
The allure of night, a tender sigh,
Where dreams take flight and fears comply.

Reflections on a Quiet Lake

A stillness rests upon the lake,
Mirroring peace with every wake.
Ripples dance with a gentle sigh,
Beneath the vast and open sky.

Cypress trees in a thoughtful pose,
Whisper tales that only nature knows.
The sun dips low, painting gold,
A serene story quietly unfolds.

Ducks glide through in graceful arcs,
Adding life to the water's marks.
Their laughter echoes, sweet and clear,
In this refuge, love draws near.

Clouds reflect in a waltzing haze,
A canvas of colors, a quiet praise.
Each moment still, time seems to freeze,
Wrapped in nature's tender ease.

As stars arrive, the lake will glow,
Twinkling back from depths below.
Reflections on a quiet lake,
Hold memories that time won't take.

Elysian Fields of Tranquility

Beneath the skies of gentle blue,
The whispers of the breeze renew.
In emerald meadows, soft and wide,
Peaceful hearts and dreams abide.

The lark sings sweet in morning's light,
While shadows dance in soft moonlight.
Here every soul finds room to breathe,
In nature's arms, we find reprieve.

Golden petals in the sun,
The warmth of laughter, stories spun.
Each flower blooms with vibrant grace,
In this enchanted, sacred space.

Time flows softly, like a stream,
Where worries fade and hopes can gleam.
With every step, we feel the ground,
A quiet joy and love profound.

So let us wander, hand in hand,
Through these vast and tranquil lands.
In Elysian fields, forever stay,
And let our spirits dance and sway.

Luminous Paths Through the Orchard

In the orchard where trees bow low,
Golden fruit in sunlit glow.
Lush grasses sway, a fragrant breeze,
Nature's bounty puts hearts at ease.

With every step on winding trails,
The scent of blossoms never fails.
Sunbeams filter through leafy crowns,
As laughter sings and joy abounds.

Beneath the branches, shadows play,
The joyful children run and sway.
Each footfall tells a tale of old,
Of summer days and dreams of gold.

In this haven, time stands still,
Where every moment, hearts can fill.
With friends beside, the world seems bright,
In orchards bathed in soft twilight.

As evening settles, stars appear,
Whispers of night linger near.
Together, we embrace the dark,
On luminous paths, we leave our mark.

The Subtle Art of Contentment

In simple things, we find delight,
A cozy nook in soft moonlight.
With every breath, we pause to see,
The beauty of just being free.

A steaming cup, warm in our hands,
The rustle of leaves in quiet strands.
Moments shared, a gentle touch,
In silence, we discover much.

The world outside may rush and roar,
Yet here, within, we ask for more.
With open hearts, we choose to stay,
In now, we weave our lives each day.

A subtle dance of joy and peace,
In every heartbeat, a sweet release.
We find our strengths in what we are,
Contentment shines, a guiding star.

So let us gather, close, and near,
Embrace the warmth, dissolve our fear.
In life's simple art, we find,
The treasure that we've long defined.

Wonders of the Calm Dawn

As dawn unfolds with softest grace,
The world awakens in its place.
With hues of gold and softest blue,
The day begins with dreams anew.

In stillness, whispers fill the air,
As nature wakes without a care.
Birds serenade the waking light,
In this embrace, all feels just right.

Each dew-kissed blade, a gem to see,
Reflects the light, a symphony.
With every moment, time is spun,
In quiet awe, we greet the sun.

The tender hues that streak the sky,
Invite our hearts to rise and fly.
With every sunrise, hope is born,
A dance of light, a new day's dawn.

So take a breath, feel life's embrace,
In calm dawn's glow, find your grace.
For wonders thrive in gentle morn,
As we awake, forever reborn.

A Drift of Flowers on Golden Paths

On golden paths the flowers sway,
Bright colors dance in light of day.
A breeze that whispers soft and low,
In gentle waves, the petals flow.

Among the blooms, the bees do hum,
With scents of nectar that they come.
Each step reveals a vibrant scene,
As nature's palette reigns supreme.

In sunlit corners shadows play,
While butterflies flit on their way.
A drift of flowers, bright and bold,
A tapestry of stories told.

With every bloom, a tale we find,
Of sunny days, love intertwined.
In harmony, the flowers bloom,
In every corner, sweet perfume.

So roam the paths where colors gleam,
And let your heart hold fast the dream.
For in this drift, the world is wide,
A lovely place where joy abides.

Starlit Reflections in Still Waters

Beneath the stars, the waters gleam,
A mirrored sky, a tranquil dream.
The moonlight dances on the lake,
In silent whispers, dreams awake.

Each ripple holds a secret bright,
The night unfolds its pure delight.
With every twinkle, shadows play,
In harmony, the night holds sway.

As constellations weave their tale,
The gentle breeze begins to sail.
In starlit grace, the waters sigh,
A peaceful world beneath the sky.

Reflections dance on crystal clear,
Embraced by silence, close and near.
In stillness, all the troubles cease,
As nature sings its song of peace.

So linger here, let moments flow,
In starlit realms, your spirit grow.
For in the night, the heart can soar,
In still waters, forevermore.

Dreamlike Journeys through Whispering Woods

In whispering woods, where shadows dwell,
The ancient trees weave tales to tell.
With every step, a secret glows,
As quiet paths where dreamers chose.

The leaves above, a emerald crown,
In soft embrace, the world slows down.
With twilight's brush, colors ignite,
In harmony, day turns to night.

Among the roots, the fairies play,
While stars peek through in soft array.
A lantern's glow, the path reveals,
As magic stirs, the heart it heals.

In those deep groves, the air is sweet,
With every echo, a heartbeat.
The whispers call with gentle grace,
To lose ourselves in nature's embrace.

So let us journey, side by side,
Through dreams and woods, where love abides.
In every step, a new refrain,
The song of life in crystal rain.

Velvet Skies and Gentle Nights

In velvet skies, the stars ignite,
Their gentle glow brings pure delight.
The world below in shadows rests,
As night unfolds its fragrant vests.

With whispers soft, the breezes sweep,
Through fields of dreams, where angels sleep.
Each moment holds a lullaby,
In gentle nights where spirits fly.

The moon, a pearl in heaven's dome,
Calls out to hearts that seek a home.
In twinkling lights, the stories blend,
As night and dreams begin to mend.

So wrap yourself in starlit grace,
Let go of time, find your own place.
In velvet skies, your worries fade,
While gentle nights, a promise made.

Embrace the stillness, breath it in,
For in this peace, we all begin.
With every night, a canvas wide,
In velvet skies, our dreams abide.

Caressing Winds and Flickering Fireflies

In twilight's glow, the breezes play,
Whispers soft as night descends.
Fireflies dance, a gentle sway,
Their glow a map that nature sends.

The world slows down, a calming sigh,
With every pulse, the heart beats free.
The sky adorned, the stars draw nigh,
In this moment, we're meant to be.

Through fields of dreams, we wander far,
Chasing shadows, we lose all care.
A symphony of light and star,
In perfect harmony, we share.

The night unveils its velvet cloak,
Embracing all beneath its grace.
In whispers sweet, the silence spoke,
In this embrace, we find our place.

As flickers fade, the dawn will rise,
Yet memories linger, warm and bright.
With every breeze and all the sighs,
We carry forth the magic night.

Timeless Peace in a Hidden Meadow

In secret glades where wildflowers bloom,
Nature paints in colors soft and bright.
The world retreats, dispelling gloom,
In this haven, hearts take flight.

Golden rays through branches filter,
Whispers of leaves in gentle sway.
A soothing calm begins to glitter,
As time stands still, a sweet delay.

Beneath the trees, I lay in dream,
The brook's soft murmur sings to me.
A perfect world, or so it seems,
Where every thought can wander free.

Clouds drift by, a slow parade,
Each breath a gift, the air so pure.
In this oasis, fears all fade,
With every moment, hearts endure.

As twilight brushes every hue,
A timeless peace enfolds the land.
In hidden meadows, life feels new,
In nature's arms, we understand.

Echoes of Laughter Beneath the Trees

Beneath the branches, joy takes flight,
Where laughter dances on the breeze.
Children's voices, pure delight,
Ring out with love beneath the leaves.

Each rustling leaf a tale to tell,
In secret corners, stories weave.
The laughter spreads like magic spell,
In every heart, it takes its leave.

Sunlight filters through the boughs,
Creating patterns on the ground.
In nature's arms, we make our vows,
To cherish each soft, loving sound.

With every moment, time stands still,
As echoes linger, pure and bright.
In unison with nature's will,
Our spirits soar, and hearts ignite.

As shadows stretch and daylight wanes,
We hold these memories close and dear.
In laughter's joy, the heart remains,
Beneath the trees, we find our cheer.

Lazy Days and Soft Sunbeams

In gentle rays, the world awakes,
With laughter woven in the breeze.
A moment's pause, the heart partakes,
Of lazy days beneath the trees.

Time drifts slow like clouds above,
With playful sounds of joy and cheer.
Nature's hug, a gift of love,
In sun-kissed laughter, all is clear.

Each soft sunbeam, a warm embrace,
A golden touch on skin and soul.
With every breath, we find our place,
In this stillness, we become whole.

The world outside may rush and race,
But here, we revel in the now.
As moments blend in perfect grace,
With nature's rhythm, we can bow.

As twilight brings its gentle close,
The sun dips low, a sweet goodnight.
In lazy days, our spirit grows,
Awash in peace, in soft twilight.

A Dance of the Fireflies

In the hush of night, they glow,
Tiny lanterns put on a show.
Whirling, twirling in the air,
A dance of dreams, light and rare.

Beneath the trees, shadows play,
Their flickering warmth invites the sway.
A chorus of whispers in the dark,
Nature's muse, a glowing spark.

Around the pond, they weave and spin,
Enticing the night, a gentle grin.
Each flash tells a story untold,
Of magic moments, bright and bold.

Their soft light reflects the stars,
Bringing peace, erasing scars.
In every flicker, a wish is made,
In this dance, our fears all fade.

As dawn approaches, they bid farewell,
Carrying secrets they will not tell.
Yet in our hearts, their light will stay,
A memory of the night's ballet.

Stars in a Quiet Sky

High above, the stars ignite,
Glimmers of hope, so pure, so bright.
Whispers of dreams in the vast unknown,
In a quiet sky, we are not alone.

Each twinkle tells a story old,
Of ancient nights and tales retold.
They guide us through the darkened hours,
Radiating soft, celestial powers.

In the stillness, we find our place,
Under the heavens, an endless embrace.
Breathtaking beauty, a silent hymn,
In the cosmic dance, we feel the whim.

The night wraps around like a shroud,
In awe, we stand, humbled, proud.
For in the vastness, we behold,
Stories written in stardust, bold.

So let us dream beneath their gaze,
In silver light, our spirits blaze.
With each heartbeat, the cosmos sighs,
Together, we'll reach for the endless skies.

The Allure of Moonlit Waters

On the silver lake, a soft glow lies,
Moonlight dances, reflecting skies.
Rippling whispers in the cool night air,
Secrets linger, both fragile and rare.

The water shimmers, a liquid dream,
As stars embrace the gentle stream.
Each wave a brushstroke, painted light,
A captivating canvas, pure delight.

Beneath the surface, shadows play,
Echoes of thoughts that drift away.
Silken reflections, the world awash,
In the stillness, time begins to blush.

Calling us gently with its allure,
A haunted beauty, wild and pure.
In the quiet, our hearts unfurl,
Lost in the magic, we take a whirl.

As night chases dawn, the waters fade,
But in our souls, the memories stayed.
For in that glow, we found our part,
A moonlit dance that touched the heart.

Embrace of the Morning Dew

As dawn approaches, the world awakes,
Whispers of light through the trees it breaks.
Delicate jewels on blades of grass,
Glistening softly as moments pass.

Each droplet holds a secret glow,
Reflecting hues of the sun's first show.
In this embrace, the earth breathes deep,
Inviting dreams from the night's sweet sleep.

Petals unfurl, kissed by the day,
Nature opens her arms, at play.
A symphony of colors, fresh and new,
The promise of life in the morning dew.

With every step, the ground does sigh,
Underfoot, where soft dreams lie.
In this gentle warmth, we find reprieve,
A moment to cherish, a chance to believe.

So as the sun climbs high and bright,
Let us hold onto this pure delight.
For in the morning, wrapped in its hue,
We find our hearts in the morning dew.

Moments of Stillness in a Busy World

In the rush of life we tread,
Silent whispers softly spread.
Time to pause, to breathe anew,
Find a moment just for you.

In crowded streets, a gentle sigh,
Underneath the azure sky.
Let your thoughts drift far away,
In stillness, find your perfect day.

A cup of tea, a quiet nook,
Pages turning in a book.
Feel the heartbeat, slow and sweet,
In the calm, let worries retreat.

Open eyes to beauty's grace,
In every glance, a sacred space.
In the chaos, stillness lies,
A haven found beneath the skies.

Moments precious, fleeting, rare,
A testament to show we care.
In this world of rush and race,
Let us cherish time's embrace.

The Magic of Soft Shadows

As daylight fades, so do the lines,
Soft shadows dance and intertwine.
Whispers of dusk, a tender call,
In dusky hues, we find our all.

The trees become a glowing screen,
Silhouettes in twilight's sheen.
Underneath the moon's soft gaze,
Life's moments wrapped in gentle haze.

A lantern's light begins to glow,
Guiding us where dreams can flow.
In the shadows, secrets dwell,
Stories that we yearn to tell.

Magic lingers in the night,
A tapestry of stars so bright.
Soft shadows whisper ancient tales,
Of lost loves and tender trails.

In every shape the shadows cast,
Echoes of the future and past.
Embrace this quiet, wondrous art,
For in the shadows, shines the heart.

Unwind in Nature's Gentle Arms

In the forest, time stands still,
Nature's song, a calming thrill.
Leaves a-buzz with life's refrain,
An embrace that eases pain.

By the stream where waters flow,
Softened heart, let worries go.
Stone and moss, a peaceful bed,
Whispered dreams, silently spread.

Breeze that carries scents so sweet,
Moments here feel so complete.
Petals fall and grass does sway,
In this place, I long to stay.

Mountains rise, a silent guard,
Nature watching, ever starred.
With each step beneath the skies,
Truth emerges, wisdom flies.

Unwind here, let the world fade,
In this calm, my fears are laid.
Nature's arms, a firm embrace,
Here I find my sacred space.

Glimmers of Dawn on Quiet Waters

As dawn awakes, a soft refrain,
Glimmers dance on waters plain.
Colors merge in gentle grace,
Nature's touch, a warm embrace.

Reflections of a waking sun,
Another day has now begun.
Mist that rises, veil so light,
Whispering secrets of the night.

Ripples sing a tranquil beat,
Inviting hearts to find their seat.
In the stillness, dreams ignite,
Hope and warmth in morning light.

Birds take flight in skies of gold,
Stories of the day unfold.
In the hush, all fears subside,
Feeling lost is cast aside.

Glimmers spark in every heart,
A brand new canvas, a fresh start.
On quiet waters, life bestows,
The gift of dawn as it bestows.

Whispers of a Gentle Breeze

Whispers dance through morning air,
Softly brushing through my hair.
Nature's voice, a sweet embrace,
A tender touch, a fleeting grace.

Every leaf begins to sway,
In the warmth of golden ray.
Rustling tales from trees so high,
Beneath the vast and open sky.

Clouds meander, drift apart,
In the rhythm, nature's heart.
With a sigh, the breezes flow,
Telling secrets only they know.

Crisp and fresh, the fragrant air,
Fills the world, beyond compare.
Whispers that make shadows dance,
In this moment, lost in chance.

Breezes carry dreams anew,
Painting skies in a vibrant hue.
With each puff, a promise brought,
In the stillness, time is caught.

Serenity in Sunlight

Sunlight spills on dewy grass,
A golden warmth, the hours pass.
In this glow, the heart finds peace,
As the world's commotion cease.

Birds sing sweetly from afar,
Beneath the canopy of stars.
Nature whispers soft and low,
In the light's enchanted glow.

Shadows dance beneath the trees,
Gentle touches in the breeze.
Every ray, a tender kiss,
Filling moments up with bliss.

Petals open, colors bright,
Filling days with pure delight.
In the tranquil light we find,
All our worries left behind.

As the sun begins to sink,
In its warmth, we stop to think.
Grateful for this day's sweet light,
In serenity, all feels right.

Laughter Among the Leaves

Laughter echoes through the trees,
Joyful whispers on the breeze.
Children play beneath the sun,
In a world where dreams are spun.

Rustling leaves, a merry tune,
Dancing shadows beneath the moon.
Nature joins the lively cheer,
As happiness draws near.

Footsteps cover forest trails,
Carried on the playful gales.
Every giggle, every shout,
Fills the air, there's no doubt.

Branches sway, a rhythmic sound,
Laughter shared, forever bound.
In these moments, hearts align,
Life entwined, a joy divine.

As twilight paints the sky with light,
Memories weave through day and night.
Among the leaves, we celebrate,
In the magic, we create.

Soft Echoes of Twilight

Twilight whispers sweetly near,
As day departs, the stars appear.
Gentle hues of purple blend,
In this hour, the world can mend.

Shadows stretch and softly play,
As the sun gives way to gray.
Every echo holds a tale,
In the calm where dreams prevail.

Birds retreat to nest and rest,
Nature sighs, its heart expressed.
In the stillness, thoughts will glide,
On the night's soft, peaceful tide.

With each star, a hope ignites,
In the cool embrace of nights.
Underneath the vast sky's dome,
We find comfort, we find home.

As the moon begins to rise,
Magic weaves through starlit skies.
In these echoes, peace unspun,
Soft goodbyes to day's bright sun.

Echoes of Soft Laughter

In the garden where dreams play,
Children's whispers softly sway,
Grasses dance to footsteps light,
Echoes fade into the night.

Joyful hearts in every sound,
A melody that spins around,
Tickled by the breeze so free,
Laughter flows like a gentle sea.

Moments shared beneath the sun,
Chasing shadows, having fun,
Simple pleasures fill the air,
Echoes linger everywhere.

Moonlight dances on the dew,
Memories of days so true,
Innocence, like petals bright,
Echoes gleam in the soft light.

Holding tight to fleeting days,
Time slips softly, sways and plays,
Yet in hearts, the laughter stays,
In the echoes of sweet praise.

Swaying Blossoms in the Air

Petals twirl on whispers low,
Caught in breezes, they gently flow,
Colors swirl like a painter's dream,
Swaying softly, a visual stream.

Underneath the vibrant trees,
Nature bends to a tender breeze,
Blossoms dance, a delicate art,
Swaying sweetly, touching the heart.

In the sunlight's warm embrace,
Every bloom finds its own place,
Fragrant scents fill the lightening air,
Swaying softly without a care.

As the seasons start to change,
Nature's beauty feels so strange,
Yet the blossoms always sway,
Holding on to joyful play.

In the twilight's gentle glow,
Swaying friends, so long they know,
Life's soft whispers always share,
Swaying blossoms kiss the air.

The Velvet of a Soft Pastel Sky

Dusk drapes velvet over the day,
Pastel hues in soft array,
Whispers of the night begin,
As light fades, dreams spill in.

Clouds gentle, like drifting cream,
Painting shadows, igniting dreams,
Colors mingle, sweetly sigh,
In the velvet of the sky.

Stars appear, a twinkling cast,
Reminding us of moments past,
Glimmers bright in twilight's lane,
In the calm, we feel the gain.

With every breath, the night unfolds,
In whispers soft, the magic holds,
Velvet dreams softly sing,
In this peace, our souls take wing.

Crickets chirp a soothing song,
In this space, we all belong,
As twilight kisses the last light,
The velvet sky greets the night.

Radiant Days of Golden Glow

Morning breaks with golden rays,
Warming hearts in countless ways,
Every shadow fades away,
In the light of a perfect day.

Flowers bloom, where sunbeams fall,
Nature echoes a joyful call,
Life awakens, vibrant and free,
Golden moments, meant to be.

Children laugh, their spirits soar,
Chasing dreams along the shore,
Every heartbeat, a beautiful flow,
In radiant days of golden glow.

Time stands still, if just for now,
Beneath the sun, we take a bow,
In every smile, the warmth we share,
Radiant love fills the air.

As evening falls, the world will rest,
Memories whisper, feeling blessed,
In the glow of all we've known,
Radiant days, forever grown.

Moonlit Caresses Over Still Waters

Beneath the glow of silver light,
Reflections dance, soft and bright.
Whispers carried on the breeze,
Nature's calm, a gentle tease.

Ripples form with every sigh,
Stars above, they seem to cry.
The night unfolds its tender grace,
In the moonlit, tranquil space.

Leaves that rustle, secrets tell,
In this quiet, tranquil shell.
Water glistens, tender kiss,
A moment wrapped in timeless bliss.

Each soft wave, a lover's dream,
Underneath the silver beam.
Whispers fade into the night,
In the dark, all feel so right.

Time slips by as shadows play,
In the stillness, hearts will sway.
Moonlit caresses, purest art,
A masterpiece that stirs the heart.

A Symphony of Gentle Murmurs

Listen close, the world awakes,
Softest sounds, the earth partakes.
Leaves that rustle, water's flow,
Nature's choir, a gentle glow.

Whispers linger in the air,
Echoing of love and care.
Birds in flight, their songs abide,
In the dawn, where dreams collide.

Rustling grasses lead the way,
Through the warmth of breaking day.
Every note a story weaves,
In the heart, where joy believes.

Clouds that drift, with breezes blend,
In this symphony, we mend.
Harmony of day and night,
A serenade, pure delight.

Let your spirit drift and glide,
On the murmurs, let it ride.
Nature's breath, a soothing balm,
In its melody, we find calm.

The Dance of the Gentle Flame

In the hearth, the embers glow,
A dance of light, soft and slow.
Fingers reach, then intertwine,
The gentle flame, a love divine.

Flickering shadows on the wall,
A silent story, captivating all.
Each jump, each sway, a graceful twist,
In the fire's warm, glowing mist.

Crisp air crisp with whispers low,
As the flame begins to grow.
A warmth that wraps, a sweet embrace,
In the darkness, find your place.

Softly crackles, longingly sings,
Of hidden dreams and offered wings.
In its heart, the secrets dwell,
In its glow, all fears dispel.

So gather 'round, let shadows fall,
As the gentle flames enthrall.
In this dance, we lose our care,
In the heat, love fills the air.

Secrets in the Sway of Grasses

Tall grasses whisper tales untold,
In the breeze, their secrets unfold.
Rustling softly, they converse,
Nature's language, calm and diverse.

In the meadows, life finds ways,
In each sway, the sunlight plays.
Dancing free, the grasses bend,
A fleeting moment, around the bend.

Each movement brings a different sound,
A tranquil world, peaceful and profound.
A canvas painted green and gold,
With stories of the earth, behold.

Swaying gently, they embrace the air,
In their dance, there's magic rare.
Roots entwined with ancient lore,
In the sway, we all explore.

Secrets kept in whispers low,
In the fields where wildflowers grow.
As the sun dips, shadows blend,
In this moment, heart will mend.

Sweet Nothings under Starlit Skies

In whispers soft, the night unfolds,
Stars twinkle bright, their secrets told.
Under the veil where dreams collide,
We share sweet nothings side by side.

The moonlight dances on your face,
In this quiet, sacred space.
With every breath, our hearts align,
Lost in the magic, yours in mine.

Murmurs play like gentle streams,
Woven softly into dreams.
The sky, a canvas, vast and deep,
In these moments, love we keep.

A breeze carries our laughter high,
Like fleeting notes that drift and fly.
Wrapped in warmth, the world goes still,
Together here, we find our will.

So lay your head upon my chest,
In this starlit night, we are blessed.
Sweet nothings under cosmic light,
Forever bound in love's delight.

Floating Clouds and Sweet Sunsets

The horizon blushes as day fades,
Colors swirl in gentle cascades.
Floating clouds in hues of gold,
Whisper secrets, stories untold.

As the sun dips low, shadows play,
Painting the sky in a vibrant array.
We watch the beauty, hand in hand,
Together lost in this dreamland.

Soft silhouettes of trees emerge,
In quiet whisper, our hearts surge.
The last light dances on your skin,
In this stillness, our love begins.

With every moment, time slows down,
We wear our joy like a crown.
Floating clouds, their soft embrace,
Carrying wishes, dreams interlace.

As twilight unfolds, stars will peek,
In silence, all the words we seek.
Sweet sunsets mark our cherished days,
In love's embrace, forever stay.

Nature's Embrace in the Evening Glow

In the evening's gentle bloom,
Nature wraps us in her womb.
Golden rays through leaves do weave,
In this moment, I believe.

Birds sing sweetly, the world at peace,
As daylight wanes, our worries cease.
Crickets chirp their lullaby,
Underneath the velvet sky.

A fragrant breeze whispers our name,
In nature's warmth, we're stoked by flame.
Hands entwined, we share a sigh,
Embraced by earth, you and I.

As the sun blinks one last time,
We sit beneath the ancient pine.
Life's chaos quiets, love takes hold,
In evening's glow, our hearts unfold.

So come, my dear, let's softly roam,
In nature's embrace, we find our home.
Under the stars, forevermore,
Evening treasures we adore.

Captivating Days of Golden Light

The dawn ignites the waking day,
With golden beams that find their way.
Moments captured, fleeting grace,
In every smile, in every face.

As laughter echoes, shadows play,
Sunshine dances, bright and gay.
Together chasing dreams so bold,
In captivating warmth we hold.

The world adorned in vibrant hues,
Nature's palette, endless views.
Time stands still with every glance,
In love's embrace, we twirl and dance.

Fields of gold stretch far and wide,
With you, my joy, I cannot hide.
As day transforms to evening's glow,
In every heartbeat, love will flow.

So cherish these days, burning bright,
In the arms of love, our guiding light.
Captivating moments, forever shared,
In golden light, we are prepared.

Tranquil Moments in Time

In the stillness of the dawn,
Echoes of life softly yawn.
Whispers linger on a breeze,
Brushing past like gentle keys.

Sunlight dances on the dew,
Painting pathways bright and new.
Nature hums a sacred tune,
Starlit dreams beneath the moon.

Every heartbeat calms the mind,
Peaceful moments intertwined.
Timeless echoes in the air,
Gentle sighs, a world laid bare.

Nature's cradle, pure and sweet,
Where the earth and silence meet.
Savoring what life bestows,
In these moments, healing flows.

Time stands still in this embrace,
At the heart of nature's grace.
Here, the soul finds its true rhyme,
Lost and found in tranquil time.

Gentle Waves of Softness

Ripples touch the sandy shore,
Caressing dreams forevermore.
Whispers of the ocean breeze,
Softly sway among the trees.

The tide reports its constant tale,
Echoing each serene exhale.
Gentle waves in ebb and flow,
Carrying secrets deep and low.

Silken skies reflect on waves,
Where the heart forever braves.
In this dance, the world unwinds,
Nature's chorus, peace it finds.

Amongst the seafoam's sweet embrace,
Time slows down, no need to race.
Every grain of sand, a spark,
Illuminating life's deep arc.

Beneath the coast's soft lullaby,
Every sorrow seems to die.
In the stillness, hearts revive,
In gentle waves, we come alive.

Enchantment Under the Pines

In the forest's deep embrace,
Whispers dance, a sacred space.
Pines stand tall, their secrets known,
Sharing tales in twilight's tone.

Moonlight filters through the leaves,
Weaving dreams the darkness weaves.
Each shadow moves with gentle grace,
In this stillness, time finds place.

Crickets serenade the night,
Cradling stars in silver light.
Echoes of the wild reside,
Magic thrums beneath the tide.

Every breath a world unveiled,
In this wonder, hearts have sailed.
Embraced by nature's sovereign hymn,
Life unfolds on whispers' whim.

Underneath the starlit skies,
Beauty lingers, never dies.
Enchanted moments softly bind,
The spirit free, the heart aligned.

Lullaby of the Evening Glow

As day recedes, a tender light,
Wraps the world in warmth tonight.
Colors bleed into the sky,
Where the weary spirits sigh.

The sun bows low, a gentle fade,
Dreams awaken, fears cascade.
In the hush of twilight's breath,
All find solace, peace in death.

Stars emerge, one by one,
Twinkling whispers of what's done.
Each heartbeat slows, embracing time,
In this moment, life's a rhyme.

Crickets tune their evening song,
Lulling all, where we belong.
Nature cradles us in bliss,
With every shadow, every kiss.

Underneath the evening glow,
Feel the magic, let it flow.
In this hush, the heart knows well,
Time and love in a soft swell.

Unwritten Stories in the Silence

In the hush of night's embrace,
Dreams linger in hidden space.
Silent echoes of the past,
Whispers of shadows, fading fast.

Pages turn without a sound,
Secrets in silence, tightly bound.
Hope weaves through the quiet air,
Moments caught, fragile and rare.

Eyes closed tight, the heart knows well,
Every story, it has to tell.
From stillness blooms a vibrant tale,
In the shadows, voices sail.

A world painted in muted hues,
Every breath, a chance to choose.
In the twilight, truths unfold,
Unseen chapters waiting, bold.

Listen close, for you will find,
The heart's language, warm and kind.
In unwritten stories, we'll reside,
In the silence, we confide.

A Gentle Touch of Twilight

In twilight's embrace, colors blend,
A gentle whisper, the day's end.
Soft shadows dance on the ground,
In this moment, peace is found.

Golden hues fade to deep blue,
As stars awaken, one by one, too.
The moon peeks shyly from behind,
An artist, painting night's design.

Cool breezes carry scents of pine,
Encircling hearts that intertwine.
A tranquil sigh, the world slows down,
In twilight's arms, love is renowned.

Last light filters through the trees,
A sacred space, a tender breeze.
Hope glimmers in the dusky glow,
As day surrenders, night will grow.

In the quiet, dreams take flight,
Guided by the soft twilight.
Embrace the magic, hold it tight,
In this moment, all feels right.

The Peace Within the Pines

Among the pines, a soft refrain,
Nature whispers, free from pain.
Boughs sway gently in the breeze,
A symphony among the trees.

Sunlight dances on the leaves,
In this haven, the heart believes.
Roots extend, they touch the ground,
In their presence, peace is found.

Cool shadows cast; the world feels still,
Perfect pause from life's swift thrill.
Each breath draws in the forest's grace,
In the quiet, there's a place.

Birdsong twirls through branches high,
Echoing soft as clouds drift by.
The world outside may rush and roar,
Yet here, tranquility we adore.

Beneath the pines, a secret lies,
A peace that lingers, never dies.
In nature's arms, lullabies sing,
A gentle heart, peace will bring.

Heartstrings of a Whispered Breeze

A whisper travels through the trees,
Carried softly on the breeze.
Each note, a memory reborn,
In nature's choir, hearts are worn.

The gentle touch upon the skin,
Awakens dreams that lie within.
As echoes sway through the night air,
An unseen thread, tender care.

Fleeting moments, sweet and brief,
Draw us close, beyond belief.
In the rustle of the leaves,
Love's refrain softly weaves.

Heartstrings tug with muted grace,
In every pause, we find our place.
The pulse of life runs deep and wide,
Carried forth with each soft tide.

Listen closely, let it speak,
In the silence, hearts can seek.
A whispered breeze, where stories flow,
Binding us in love's gentle glow.

Milton Keynes UK
Ingram Content Group UK Ltd.
UKHW021358081224
452111UK00007B/101